Cooking with the Danes

by Astrid Slebsager

HØST & SØNS FORLAG
COPENHAGEN

© Høst & Søns Forlag 1978.
4th printing 1988.
Translated by Paula Hostrup-Jessen.
Colour photographs by Carsten Nordholdt
(Gutenberghus Foto) and Lavinia Press.
Cover designed by Peter Lind.
Printed in Denmark by Louisetryk, Greve 1988.

ISBN 87-14-28592-4

FRONTISPIECE:
bottom: South Jutland Sour Rib (p. 71); middle: Potatoes in
White Sauce (p. 42); top: Danish Doughnuts (p. 72).

Contents

*Unless otherwise indicated
the quantities given are
for six persons.*

Foreword

Traditional Danish cookery is not normally regarded as gastronomy in the top class, but if we ask ourselves what gastronomy really is, we find it to be the art of obtaining the best result out of the available ingredients.

Gastronomy or not – good and tasty food is made in Denmark, where experience has taught us not only the finer points of cookery but how to judge the quality and potentialities of the raw materials.

Nor is gastronomy in Denmark confined to either men or women. Whether for pleasure or for practical reasons – as, for example, where both partners have jobs outside the home – cooking in many Danish homes is a co-operative venture. Frequently, the preparing and cooking of the more complicated, traditional dishes – often cheap as well as tasty – may indeed be a family affair. Thus old traditions are carried on.

Any tourist who – tired of international menus in large, impersonal hotels – may have discovered the small, intimate restaurants where truly Danish food is served, will be sure to recognize many of the recipes in this book. Moreover, a search through the book may even reveal new recipes that speedily become an integral part of a personal repertoire!

Astrid Slebsager

Winter and January

The Danish cuisine has many excellent traditions of which the Danes at any rate are very proud, and although – as a result of tinned and frozen foods and imports from sunnier climates – the seasons have lost the significance they once had, Danish eating habits are still influenced by the seasons and festivals.

This book is therefore marked by the rhythm of the seasons seen with Danish eyes. In order to dispel the gloom and sleet of January many Danes prefer to stay indoors and combat the weather, either alone or in the company of good friends, with the aid of a tasty and satisfying dish.

Burning love BRÆNDENDE KÆRLIGHED

We start the winter recipes with this traditional – and very cheap – dish.

2–2¹/₂ lb (1 kg) floury potatoes	About ¹/₂ pint (3 dl) cream	3 onions
1¹/₂–2 oz (40–50 g) butter	8–10 thick rashers of fat bacon	Salt White pepper Pinch of nutmeg

Peel and cut up the potatoes. Cook until tender in unsalted water, drain and mash. Whip in the butter gradually, and finally the cream, until the mashed potato is light and airy. Season with salt, pepper and nutmeg.

Cut the rashers and onions into small cubes and fry until crisp in a little of the bacon fat. Pile the mashed potatoes into a dish. Scoop out a hollow in the middle, pour in the fat and sprinkle with onion and bacon cubes.

Oxtail stew OKSEHALERAGOUT

Here is another tasty and substantial dish, which is also economical.

2 ox-tails	1 onion	Salt
5–6 oz (150 g)	3 leeks	Black pepper
butter	3 carrots	Flour
4 shallots	1 tin tomatoes	

Divide the ox-tails at the joints, cutting away superfluous fat. Slice the vegetables finely (except the tomatoes) and cook slowly in half the butter in a casserole until the onions are transparent.

Coat the meat in seasoned flour, brown in the remainder of the butter in a frying-pan and add to the casserole with the vegetables. Boil out the frying-pan with a little water and pour the gravy into the casserole. Break up the tomatoes and add together with the juice, adding sufficient water to cover the meat. Simmer under a tightly-fitting lid for about 2 hours, or until the meat literally falls off the bones.

Serve with mashed potato.

✓ Beer-bread ØLLEBRØD

Beer-bread is a very old and typically Danish dish, known to small children as soon as they can handle a spoon. But not only children thrive on the daily portion of beer-bread (prepared without the strong beer); there are also many adult Danes who know of no better start to the day than their morning beer-bread.

1 lb (450 g) rye-bread	3–4 tablesp. (100 g) sugar	About ¼ pint (1–2 dl) lager
1½–1¾ pints (¾ l) water	2–3 teasp. grated lemon-peel	
1½ bottles dark low-alcohol beer	Small piece of cinnamon stick	

Cut up the bread into squares and soak overnight in just sufficient cold water to cover. Simmer under a tightly-fitting lid until very soft, stirring frequently in order to prevent burning. Add water if necessary. Pass the bread soup through a sieve or blend in a mixer, return to the pot and dilute with the low-alcohol beer. Add the sugar, lemon-peel and cinnamon to taste. Simmer for 10–15 min.

If the beer-bread is too thick, dilute with water or beer, using lager if a strong flavour of beer is desired. Serve with ice-cold milk, cream or whipped cream.

Signs of Spring

Having reached the end of January, February already heralds signs of Spring – and what could be more pleasing to Danish eyes!

Jellied lumpfish STENBIDER I GELÉ

The lumpfish is a sure sign of Spring. The saying goes that when it loosens its hold on the stone, deep down in the water – and that is generally in February – there are only six weeks of Winter left, and so the lumpfish is greatly prized here in the cold North.

1 male lumpfish with sucking disc, liver and soft roe	1 part vinegar to 2–4 parts water 1 small sliced onion	Salt Lemon Parsley or dill Gelatine
1 sliced carrot	12–15 peppercorns	Egg-whites

Ask the fishmonger to clean and remove the skin. Place in sufficient water and vinegar to cover together with the salt, pepper and vegetables. Bring slowly to the boil and simmer for 10–12 min. according to size.

Cook the sucking disc, liver and roe separately in slightly salted water, removing as they become tender. Drain. Take out the fish when cooked and pluck the flesh from the bones in large pieces. Place in a bowl or ring mould in layers alternatively with pieces of liver, roe and sucking disc.

Boil up the liquid, remove the scum and sieve through a clean linen cloth wrung out in boiling water. If still not clear, cool and beat in one egg-white per pint ($^1/_2$ l) of liquid. Bring to the boil, whipping constantly. Remove the scum, sieve and cool.

Stiffen the liquid with gelatine according to the instructions on the packet, using proportionally more if the lumpfish is to be turned out of a mould. Greasing the mould with vegetable oil before filling facilitates the turning out.

Serve with lemon boats, chopped parsley or dill and home-made rye-bread and butter. See colourplate opposite page 16.

Rye-bread RUGBRØD

Rye-bread is typically Danish, and just as staple an item in Danish housekeeping as the baguette in French. Obtainable from any Danish baker's shop or grocery, it may be difficult to get abroad, so here is the recipe:

$3^1/_2$ oz (100 g) yeast	3–4 tablesp. (1 dl) water	1 teasp. salt
1 pint (5 dl) buttermilk	About $1^3/_4$ lb (850 g) rye flour	3 cl. aquavit, if desired

All the ingredients should preferably be at room temperature before baking.

Heat the buttermilk and water until lukewarn (35°

11

C), stir in the yeast and gradually add the salt and flour. Knead until smooth and shiny, adding a little more water if necessary. Cover with a damp cloth and leave to rise in a warm place for 2 hours with no draught.

When risen, knead lightly, transfer to a greased form and set aside for 1 hour to rise again, covering with a damp cloth. Brush with water and bake at 400° F (200° C) for about 1¼ hr, brushing now and again with water during the baking.

The aquavit in the dough does not impart any flavour but helps the bread to remain fresh. See colourplate opposite page 16.

Shrovetide

In Denmark, as in other Catholic countries before the Reformation, Shrovetide heralded the beginning of Lent, which lasted until Good Friday. Although Lent was abolished in Denmark, the Shrovetide traditions and jollities lived on.

Originally Shrovetide was an old heathen Spring festival, and must have had a special attraction for the Danes, since it is still celebrated today as the custom of tilting at a barrel – supposedly containing a cat. In olden days it was sheer cruelty to animals, since there was in fact a cat in the barrel!

Carneval, too, has still survived, although this custom is slowly dying out. The word "carneval" comes from Roman times and is the Latin for "meat" (carne) and "farewell" (vale). That is to say, "carneval" meant a "farewell to meat" – though fish was permitted instead!

Until the time of the Reformation, Shrovetide consisted of a grand spread preceding the Fast. Today the excesses are restricted to pastries like pretzels and Shrovetide buns.

Caraway seed pretzels
KOMMENSKRINGLER

1 oz (30 g) yeast	About 1¹/₄ lb
¹/₂ pint (3 dl) milk	flour (500 g)
3¹/₂ oz (100 g) butter	1 teasp. salt
	3 tablesp. caraway seeds

Dissolve the yeast in the luke-warm milk, melt the butter and add together with the flour, salt and caraway seeds, saving a few of the latter for decoration. Knead the dough until soft and shiny, leave to rise in a warm place for 45 min. covered with a damp cloth. Knead again lightly, roll into thin strips and form into pretzels. Drop them one by one into a pan of boiling water, taking them out when they rise to the surface and placing them on a greased baking-sheet. Brush with egg, sprinkle with caraway seeds and brush again. Bake at 480° F (250° C) for about 15 minutes.

Alternatively, the pretzels may be left to rise for the second time on the baking-sheet for 20 min., but the old-fashioned method with the boiling water makes them lighter.

Shrove pretzels FASTEKRINGLER

Bake according to the previous recipe, but omit the caraway seeds.

Shrove stars STRUTTER

These used to be eaten on Shrove Monday, as a first course, with hot milk and cinnamon mixed with

14

sugar, but this custom has completely died out. Nowadays they are served with coffee or tea.

The recipe is the same as for the pretzels, but a teaspoon of sugar is added to the dough.

When the dough has risen for the first time, roll it out into a long strip, divide into suitable lengths and form into buns. Cut a deep cross in each and stretch the corners so formed outwards. Turn the resulting stars upside-down and place on a greased baking-sheet, cover, and leave to rise for 15 min. Brush with beaten egg and bake at 440° F (225° C) for about 15 min.

Shrovetide buns FASTELAVNSBOLLER

Finally, these delicious Shrovetide buns, though difficult to knead, are well worth the effort.

4¹/₂ oz (125 g) butter	*¹/₂ teasp. salt*	*1 oz (30 g) raisins*
9 oz (250 g) flour	*1 oz (25 g) yeast*	*1 oz (30 g) mixed peel*
1 rounded tablesp. (35 g) sugar	*3–4 tablesp. (1 dl) milk*	
	2 small eggs	

Rub the butter into the flour, add the salt and sugar. Dissolve the yeast in the luke-warm milk, then beat the eggs and stir into the flour together with the milk and yeast. Mix well with a spoon.

Knead the dough until smooth and shiny, adding the raisins and the chopped mixed peel. Cover wih a damp cloth and leave to rise in a warm place for about 45 minutes.

Divide the dough into 10 portions and form these into

buns. Place these on a greased baking-sheet and leave to rise for 15–20 min. Brush with beaten egg and bake at 480° F (250° C) for about ¹/₂ hour.

The buns may be eaten whole, or halved and buttered.

OPPOSITE: *Jellied Lumpfish (p. 10); top left: Caraway Loaf (p. 30); top right: Rye-Bread (p. 11).*

Still Winter

Easter is still a long way off, and February and March are often very cold months in Denmark, so the nourishing, country-style dishes are extremely welcome.

White cabbage is a familiar ingredient of Danish cooking, and two of the most popular recipes are browned cabbage with pork and stuffed cabbage. Despite the more recent influence of foreign cooking, these dishes turn up at regular intervals in most Danish homes.

Browned cabbage with pork
BRUNKÅL MED FLÆSK

1 firm white cabbage (3–4 lb or 1¹/₂–2 kg)	1–2 teasp. sugar
	2 oz (50 g) butter
2 lb (1 kg) pork or fresh bacon for boiling	About ¹/₄ pint (1–1¹/₂ dl) stock
	Salt
1–2 pig's hocks	Black peppercorns

Cover the pork and the cleaned hocks with cold, slightly salted water. Bring to the boil and remove the scum. Boil up the meat for a couple of minutes, remove and rinse in cold water.

Discarding the coarse, outer leaves, quarter the cabbage and shred finely. Melt the sugar in a thick-bottomed saucepan (not aluminium) until it begins to froth, add the butter and stir over a gentle heat until toffee-coloured. Add the shredded cabbage and turn with a wooden spoon until light brown. Pack the pork and hocks into the cabbage so that they are well-covered on all sides. Add the stock and 20–25 peppercorns and simmer over a gentle heat for about 2 hours until tender, adding a little more liquid if necessary.

Season with salt and serve with rye-bread and strong mustard.

Bom BOM

Brown cabbage and pork may appear too substantial, especially for small children. In that event use force-meat instead of pork and hocks, and call the dish BOM.

It is difficult to trace the origin of this name, but it may be found in many cookery-books before the turn of the century and was probably devised by mothers wishing to entice their children to eat by inventing funny names.

1 firm white cabbage (2–3 lb or 1–1¹/₂ kg)	*About ³/₄ pint (4 dl) milk or water*	*Salt*
1 lb (¹/₂ kg) lean pork	*1 egg*	*Ground black pepper*
1 lb (¹/₂ kg) beef or veal	*2–3 tablesp. (75 g) flour*	
	1 large onion	

Prepare the cabbage as in the previous recipe.

Mince the meat (if not already minced) together with the onion and beat all the ingredients together in a mixer, if available. When beating by hand it is easiest to beat the egg and liquid separately, afterwards adding it to the meat alternatively with the flour and spices.

Leave the forcemeat in a cold place for at least 20 min. Form into a ball and pack it down into the light brown cabbage. Simmer under a tightly-fitting lid for about 1–1½ hours until tender, testing the forcemeat with a knitting-needle.

Serve as for the previous recipe. For children who do not like cabbage, serve boiled potatoes with the forcemeat.

Stuffed cabbage
FYLDT HVIDKÅL

1 firm white cabbage (3–4 lb or 1½–2 kg)	2 oz (50 g) butter
About 1 lb (500 g) forcemeat (see page 18)	About 1 pint (½ l) stock
2 tablesp. (50 g) flour	Nutmeg
	Salt
	Ground white pepper
	Cream

Discard the coarse outer leaves of the cabbage and remove the stem. Cut off a lid from the place where the stem previously was and hollow out the cabbage with a grape-fruit knife so that about 1 inch (2 cm) remains as a shell. Stuff with the forcemeat to which a little nutmeg has been added until ³/₄ of the hollow has been filled. Close with the lid, binding tightly in all directions with cotton.

Place the stuffed cabbage with lid uppermost in a large saucepan and fill with cold water until just under the lid. Sprinkle with salt and bring to the boil. Simmer for about 2 hours until tender, testing the forcemeat with a knitting needle and adding more water if necessary.

Make a white sauce with the butter, flour and cabbage stock, flavouring with nutmeg, salt and pepper and, if liked, a little cream. Serve with rye-bread and mustard.

Easter

Lamb and eggs are traditional Easter dishes. The former is derived from the Jewish Passover festival, at which lamb was roasted on a spit and eaten with unleavened bread outside in the Temple courtyard to the accompaniment of the religious rituals.

Saddle of lamb and cucumber salad
DOBBELT LAMMERYG MED AGURKESALAT

According to tradition, Easter Sunday is brought to a close with a loin of lamb – the double loin, or saddle, being an extra special delicacy. In Denmark we often eat lambs from Iceland and Greenland as well as our own, since it has a very fine quality.

About 4 lb (2 kg) saddle of lamb, preferably including the tail Salt	Ground black pepper About ³/₄ pint (3¹/₂–4 dl) stock or bouillon	2¹/₂–3 oz (75 g) butter 5–7 tablesp. (1¹/₂– 2 dl) cream Soy Sauce

Score the joint finely from side to side without cutting into the meat. Sprinkle with salt and pepper, rub with butter and brown at 480° F (250° C) in a roasting-pan for about 15–20 min. Turn down the oven to 340° F (170° C), adding about half the stock.
Roast for a good hour, testing with a knitting needle.

If the juice that runs out is pink, then the joint is done. If necessary add more liquid while roasting to prevent it from drying up. Pour the gravy into a small saucepan, add the cream and boil up, flavouring with salt, pepper and soy sauce. Meanwhile, keep the joint hot in the oven with the door ajar.

Serve with cucumber salad and small potatoes boiled in their skins, peeled, and sprinkled with parsley.

Cucumber salad
AGURKESALAT

1 cucumber	2 tablesp. water
3 teasp. salt	1 tablesp. sugar
2 tablesp. vinegar	Pinch of pepper

Wash and slice the cucumber finely. Sprinkle with salt and press between two plates for about 10 min. Thereafter squeeze out the surplus liquid and place in a marinade previously prepared by boiling the vinegar, water, sugar and pepper together and allowing to cool. Leave in a cold place for about two hours before serving.

If, instead of vinegar, lemon juice is preferred, do not boil the marinade but stir in the sugar until dissolved.

Hard-boiled eggs in mustard sauce
SKIDNE ÆG

Good Friday is traditionally a day of sorrow, and in Danish homes it was customary to eat the dullest food possible – in some regions, porridge made of rye-flour. In other places, however, this rather more

22

imaginative – and tasty – dish was preferred. For that very reason hard-boiled eggs in mustard sauce has survived a. a dish eaten not solely at Easter.

The egg, as symbol, has been handed down from the old pagan fertility rites, celebrated at roughly the same time as Easter.

8–12 eggs	l) milk	Salt
2 oz (50 g) butter	5–6 tablesp. (1–	Fish mustard (a
2 tablesp. (50 g)	1¹/₂ dl cream)	coarsely ground
flour	Ground white	mustard – see
About 1 pint (¹/₂	pepper	below)

Boil the eggs 6–7 minutes – the whites should then be firm, the yolks still a little soft.

Make a white sauce in a thick-bottomed saucepan from the butter, flour and milk, cooking well through. Gradually add the cream until a suitable consistency is obtained, seasoning with salt, pepper and fish-mustard. Pour the sauce over the shelled, hard-boiled eggs and serve with home-made rye-bread.

Fish-mustard is also known as water-ground mustard, because the mustard seed once used to be ground with a cannon ball in a clay bowl containing just enough water to hold the mustard together. Now-adays a pestle and mortar may be used instead.

The dish may also be prepared with ordinary German or French Dijon mustard, although the result is not quite the same.

Coloured eggs FARVEDE ÆG

As far as we know, there were no special dishes for Easter Saturday, but part of the day at any rate was spent in colouring eggs for Easter Sunday. The coloured eggs were once used for childrens' conjuring games. Country children used to go from farm to farm "singing for" the coloured eggs on Easter Saturday, although they were not used for conjuring until Easter Sunday.

One of the best methods of colouring eggs is with onion peel, which produces shades ranging from pale yellow to dark brown depending on how long the peel is boiled. The yellow and brown eggs used to be the most popular of the coloured eggs for Easter, not least because onions were always at hand.

Boil the peel of 2–3 onions in slightly salted water for a couple of minutes. Add the first batch of eggs and boil in the liquid until they turn yellow and are hardboiled. Remove and add the next batch, which will turn somewhat darker in colour, and so on, until the final batch is coloured a dark brown. The beautiful colours are enhanced by rubbing the coloured eggs with a piece of pork crackling until shiny. Red eggs of various shades were obtained by boiling them in beetroot vinegar – another traditional method. But later on it was discovered that still more shades could be obtained by wrapping the eggs in variously coloured tissue-paper, whereafter they were boiled – one colour at a time – in slightly salted water.

Nowadays special egg dyes with a great range of colours are obtainable, but one thing is quite sure – the best result is still obtained by rubbing with crackling!

Danish omelette ÆGGEKAGE

Finally, here are some egg dishes that make an ideal lunch.

16 rashers streaky bacon	6–8 eggs	Ground black pepper
2–3 teasp. cornflour	About ¹/₃ pint (2–2¹/₂ dl) cream	Finely chopped chives
	Salt	

Fry the bacon until crisp. Save the fat and wipe the pan clean with paper.

Beat the eggs together with the cornflour beaten up in the cream, seasoning with salt and pepper. Since the omelette is to be fried in bacon fat, do not overdo the salt.

Pour a little bacon fat into the pan and add the egg mixture. Leave it to set over a gentle heat, raising the edges from time to time to allow the egg to run down into the hot pan.

When nearly set, decorate with the bacon and sprinkle with chives. Serve directly from the pan with wholemeal rye-bread and mustard.

Instead of bacon, filleted smoked herrings may be used. In this case fry the egg mass in a little butter.

Raw beef and egg TARTAR

About 1 lb (400 g) lean beef (choose a good quality that has not been hung too long).

Rye-bread	Onion rings	Capers
Butter	Freshly grated horseradish	Chopped onion
Egg yolks		

25

Scrape the meat off the sinews with a short, sharp knife and spread the slices of buttered rye-bread with a half-inch (1 cm) layer of meat. Make a hollow in the centre, circle it with an onion ring and place a raw egg yolk in each.

Decorate with the horseradish, capers and chopped onion.

Minced beefsteak HAKKEBØF

This is one of the hot lunch dishes often served with the Danish Cold Table, but it can equally well be served for dinner.

2 lb (1 kg) minced beef	About 3 oz (75 g) butter	8–10 eggs About 1/4 pint (1–
2 tablesp. cream	Salt	11/2 dl) bouillon
4 large or 6 medium onions	Ground black pepper	

Knead the meat together with the cream and divide into suitable portions, forming them into flat, oval or round patties.

Peel the onions, chop finely and fry in one third of the butter until golden brown. Add a little of the bouillon to keep them soft, turn into an oven-proof dish and keep hot.

Boil out the pan and dry with paper. Season the beefsteaks with salt and pepper and fry in half the remaining butter for 4 min. on each side. They should remain pink inside. Serve in an oven-proof dish. Boil up the onion with a little more bouillon and distribute over the meat.

Fry the eggs in the rest of the butter and place one on

each steak. Use the remainder of the bouillon to boil
out the pan, and pour the gravy into the dish with
the meat.

Serve with rye-bread

Nine-cabbage NIKÅL

Apart from the familiar Easter traditions common to
many nations, the Danes have their own special
culinary traditions where Easter is concerned. Such
an example is Nine-cabbage, which was traditionally
eaten on Maundy Thursday in order to ensure good
health for the rest of the year. Perhaps the winter
deficit of Vitamin C was built up again with this dish.
Nine-cabbage is common kale mixed with dandelion
leaves, ground elder, chervil, parsley, chives, lovage,
thyme and leek tops – or any other young green
leaves to hand.

Ham and stewed kale
KOGT, RØGET SKINKE MED GRØNLANGKÅL

It is traditional to serve this dish on Maundy Thursday, but it may also be enjoyed out of season.

1 boneless, lightly smoked ham held together
with string (about 3 lb or 1¹/₂ kg)

Cover the ham with cold water and bring to the boil.
Simmer 25–40 min. according to thickness, and
leave to cool down in the soup. It may also be cooked
a couple of days beforehand and kept cold in the
soup. Eaten hot, it should first be removed from the

soup – which is brought to the boil – and then re-
placed and reheated in the soup for 6–8 min.

Stewed kale
GRØNLANGKÅL

3 sticks kale	³/₄ pint (4 dl)	Salt
2 oz (50 g) butter	milk	Ground white
2 tablesp. (50 g)	4–5 tablesp. cream	pepper
flour	(1–1¹/₂ dl)	Grated nutmeg

Pluck the leaves from the stalk and ribs, rinse well
and steam for ¹/₂ hour without adding more water.
Drain and pass through the mincer, or blend.
Make a white sauce with the butter, flour and milk,
add the cream and season with salt, pepper and nutmeg. Gradually stir the sauce into the kale until the
mixture has a suitable consistency and is a beautiful
dark green. Season again if necessary and serve with
the ham and potatoes browned in sugar.

Potatoes browned in sugar
BRUNEDE KARTOFLER

2 lb (1 kg) small round potatoes	2 tablesp. (50 g) sugar
	2 oz (50 g) butter

Wash, boil and peel the potatoes. Melt the sugar in a
hot pan until frothy, add the butter and stir until
smooth.
Rinse the potatoes under cold, running water and
place them in the caramel, turning with a wooden
spoon or shaking the pan until all are brown. See
colourplate opposite page 64.

28

Spring in May

At last, having reached the month of May, we can offer a number of Danish specialities of which we are justly proud. This is the season for the small fjord shrimps, not to mention asparagus and the first new potatoes. The latter are grown in sandy soil on the island of Samsø in the Kattegat, and are always the first Danish new potatoes on the market.

Shrimps
REJER

2 lb (1 kg) small shrimps	1 teasp. paprika (edelsüss)
About 5 pints (3 l) water	4–5 tablesp. cooking salt
	Dill

Rinse the shrimps under the cold tap and drain. Bring the water, salt, paprika and dill to the boil and add the shrimps. Stir with the handle of a wooden spoon until all the shrimps have changed colour and simmer for 1–2 min. according to size, leaving them to cool down in the liquid.

Serve with caraway seed bread, butter and a spray of dill. Peel the shrimps beforehand – or make a party of it by peeling them at the table.

Caraway loaf
SURBRØD

2 oz (50 g) yeast
$^1/_2$ pint ($2^1/_2$ dl)
  buttermilk
3–4 tablesp. (1 dl)
  water
14 oz (400 g)
  bolted rye-meal

About 2 teasp.
  salt
2–3 tablesp.
  caraway seeds
1 egg white

Crumble the yeast and stir into the luke-warm butter-milk. Add the water, flour, salt and about 2 tablesp. caraway seeds.

Knead the dough until smooth and shiny, cover with a damp cloth and leave to rise in a warm place for about 50–60 min.

Knead again lightly and form into a loaf. Cover and leave to rise for about 45 min. on a greased baking sheet.

Make some parallel cuts on the top surface of the loaf to let out the air, brush with egg-white beaten up with a little water, sprinkle with caraway seeds and brush again. Bake at 440° F (225° C) for about 40–45 min. See colourplate opposite page 16.

Choice asparagus
SLIKASPARGES

4 lb (2 kg)
  asparagus
4–5 pints ($2^1/_2$–

3 l) water
About 1 teasp.
  salt

Wash and peel the asparagus from the head down-wards, cutting away the last inch of stem with all the strings attached. Drop into boiling salted water

and cook from 15–18 min. according to thickness. It should remain crisp when cooked.
Serve with whipped or cold butter.

Green asparagus
GRØNNE ASPARGES

4 lb (2 kg) green asparagus 4–5 pints (2¹/₂–3 l	water About 1 teasp. salt

Rinse, but do not peel. Instead, slice off the end of the stalk and boil in salted water for 8–10 min. It should retain its crispness.
Serve hot with whipped or cold butter, or if cold with a dressing of oil and vinegar.

Fried hornfish and parsley
STEGT HORNFISK MED PERSILLE

Another May speciality is hornfish. This may be prepared in many different ways. It may, for example, be jellied as for lumpfish (see page 10), but since it has own jellifying properties it needs less gelatine than in the recipe for lumpfish.
Here is another very simple Spring-like recipe:

3 lb (1¹/₂ kg) hornfish Flour Salt	Ground white pepper Parsley	3–4 oz (100 g) butter 2 lemons

Clean the fish, cut off the fins and remove the bones. Rinse and pat dry with kitchen paper and cut into 3–4 inch (8–10 cm) pieces. Roll each piece around a sprig of parsley, fastening with a skewer, and turn in seasoned flour. Fry the fish in browned butter for 3–4 min. on each side until white and firm.

Serve with small potatoes – cooked in their skins, peeled and sprinkled with parsley – browned butter, lemon boats and cucumber salad made with lemon juice.

New potatoes NYE KARTOFLER

The first new potatoes of the season are a great delicacy, especially those from the Danish island of Samsø. All new potatoes, however, should be treated with respect. Rub them between the fingers until clean, rinsing in cold water, and drop them into boiling, salted water and simmer until not quite cooked. Drain off the water and steam gently until soft, **shaking** from time to time.

June and Summer

This time we shall reverse the procedure and start with a sweet in celebration of Denmark's Constitution Day, which is the fifth of June.

Constitution pudding
GRUNDLOVSDESSERT

1 lb (500 g) wine rhubarb	¹/₂ vanilla pod
About 3 tablesp. (100 g) sugar	1 envelope or ¹/₂ oz (15 g) powered gelatine
4 eggs	
¹/₂–³/₄ pint (4 dl) whipping cream	Almonds for decoration

Wash and cut the rhubarb into 1 inch (2 cm) pieces. Place in an oven-proof dish and sprinkle with sugar to taste. As soon as the juice forms, cover and bake at 350° F (175° C) for 20–25 min. or until tender.

Meanwhile, prepare the egg-custard. Whip the egg-yolks with 2–3 tablesp. sugar until white and fluffy. Boil up half the cream with the vanilla pod until it has imparted its flavour, and beat gradually into the egg mixture. Prepare the gelatine according to the instructions on the packet and stir into the custard, continuing to stir until it begins to set. Beat and fold in the egg-whites. Whip the remainder of the cream and stir in about half.

Pour the fruit into a bowl, saving a few pieces for

decoration, and pour the custard over it. Leave until quite stiff, and decorate with whipped cream, pieces of rhubarb and sliced almonds.

✓ Lamb chops and spinach
LAMMEKOTELETTER MED SPINAT

Lamb chops make an excellent first course to go with Constitution Pudding.

12–16 lambcutlets	Rosemary	Small new
Salt	Butter for frying	potatoes
Ground black	4 lb (2 kg)	
pepper	spinach	

Beat the cutlets lightly, season with salt and pepper and – if the cutlets are not too delicate – with a little rosemary. Fry in browned butter for about 2 min. on each side. They should be pink inside when cooked.

Spinach SPINAT

Wash the spinach, removing the stalks and coarse veins. Steam without adding any more water, drain well and place in the pan with the browned butter. Turn until hot through, adding a little more butter and seasoning if necessary. Serve the lamb cutlets and spinach with new potatoes.

Cauliflower au gratin BLOMKÅLSGRATIN

Another dish for May and June, popular in Danish homes.

34

1 large cauliflower	About ³/₄ pint (3¹/₂–4 dl) water in which the cauliflower has been boiled	¹/₄–¹/₂ pint (2 dl) milk
5 oz (150 g) butter		Salt
5 oz (150 g) flour	7 eggs	Ground white pepper
		Grated nutmeg
		2 teasp. cornflour

Divide the cauliflower into sprigs. Soak in salt water for a while and rinse well. Boil up in slightly salted water.

Make a white sauce with the butter, flour and milk, adding enough cauliflower water to make a soft, smooth dough. Allow to cool slightly and beat in the egg-yolks one by one. Finally, fold in the stiffly beaten egg-white to which the cornflour has been added.

Season to taste and line the bottom of a ovenproof dish with the gratin mixture. Add the cauliflower and pour over the remainder of the gratin mixture. Bake at 350° F (175° C) for about 1 hour, testing with a knitting needle.

Serve with cold or melted butter.

Boiled salted saddle of pork and spring cabbage
KOGT, SPRÆNGT SVINEKAM
MED SPIDSKÅL

3 lb (1¹/₂ kg) salted saddle of pork

Cover with cold water and bring slowly to the boil. Simmer for 25–45 min. according to thickness, testing with a knitting needle. If the meat is allowed to overcook, it becomes stringy.

Steamed spring cabbage
DAMPET SPIDSKÅL

3–4 spring cabbages	5 oz (150 g) butter
Salt	Grated nutmeg

Discarding the coarse outer leaves, quarter the cabbages and remove the stems. Wash well in slightly salted water and steam for about 15 minutes under a tightly-fitting lid until just tender, adding a lump of butter but no further water. Sprinkle with nutmeg before serving.

Serve with the boiled pork, strong mustard and ryebread.

Spring cabbage in white sauce
STUVET SPIDSKÅL

2 oz (50 g) butter	Salt
2 oz (50 g) flour	Ground white
³/₄ pint milk (4 dl)	pepper
2–3 tablesp. cream	Pinch of nutmeg

Prepare the cabbage as above, slice and steam under a tightly-fitting lid without adding more water.

Make a white sauce with the butter, flour and milk, and add sufficient cream to produce the desired consistency. Season and add the steamed cabbage. Heat until warm through.

Fried plaice and parsley sauce
STEGTE RØDSPÆTTER MED PERSILLESOVS

Plaice are at their largest and firmest in June and July.

3 lb (1¹/₂ kg)	Ground white
plaice	pepper
Flour	Butter for frying
Salt	

Wash the plaice and remove the skin. Divide into two along the mid-line or cut into 3 pieces transversely. Coat in seasoned flour and fry in browned butter 3–4 min. on each side until white and firm right down to the bone.

Parsley sauce
PERSILLESOVS

1¹/₂ oz (40 g)	³/₄ pint (4 dl)
butter	milk
1¹/₂ tablesp. (40	3–4 tablesp. cream
g) flour	Parsley

Make a white sauce with the butter, flour and milk, adding sufficient cream to provide the required consistency. Add finely chopped parsley – enough to turn the sauce a brilliant grass-green – and season with salt.

Alternatively, the plaice may be turned in seasoned flour, dipped in beaten egg, or egg-white to which a little water has been added, and then coated in breadcrumbs.

When steaming plaice, do not remove the skin, but scrape well, rub with kitchen salt and steam in a fish-steamer. A single plaice may be steamed between two plates with a lump of butter, salt and pepper. If placed on top of the saucepan in which the potatoes are boiling, both fish and potatoes should be ready at the same time.

Pot-roasted chickens and salad
GRYDESTEGTE KYLLINGER MED SALAT

3 chickens (3–4 lb or 1¹/₂–2 kg)	¹/₂ pint (2¹/₂ dl) stock
Parsley	Butter for frying
2¹/₂–3 oz (75 g) butter	About ¹/₂ pint (2–2¹/₂ dl) cream
Salt	Soy Sauce
Ground black pepper	Cornflour

Clean the chickens, singe, and dry the insides with paper. Rub both outside and inside with salt and pepper and stuff with coarsely chopped parsley mixed with butter. Close with a skewer.

Brown the chickens in the butter, first on the breast and then on the back. Add about half the stock and pot-roast for ³/₄–1 hour, or until the legs are tender. Baste now and again, adding more liquid if necessary.

Take out the chickens, part at the joints and keep hot in an ovenproof dish covered with foil.

Boil up the gravy with a little more stock, add the cream, soy sauce and seasoning to taste and thicken with 1–2 teasp. cornflour dissolved in a little cream. Serve with new potatoes sprinkled with parsley and green salad in cream dressing.

Green salad in cream dressing
GRØN SALAT I FLØDEDRESSING

1–2 lettuces	About ¹/₃ pint (2¹/₂ dl) cream
1 egg-yolk	Juice of ¹/₂ lemon
Sugar to taste	

Wash and dry the lettuce leaves. Beat the egg-yolk with the sugar, stir in the cream and finally the lemon juice. Stir until thick.

Toss the lettuce in the dressing just before serving.

Strawberry jelly JORDBÆRGRØD

The Danish strawberry season is from the end of June until the middle of July, when the raspberry season begins. At first preferred 'au naturel', with cream, the last strawberries of the season are often made into a soft jelly – a popular method for many other summer fruits.

2 lb (1 kg) strawberries	2–3 tablesp. sugar
1/3 pint (2–2 1/2 dl) water	1–2 tablesp. cornflour

Prepare the strawberries, cover with cold water and bring slowly to the boil. Simmer for 2–3 min. until they collapse, then add the sugar to taste.

Thicken with cornflour dissolved in a little cold water. Turn into a bowl and sprinkle with sugar to prevent a skin forming.

Serve with cream or milk.

Gooseberry jelly
STIKKELSBÆRGRØD

2 lb (1 kg) green gooseberries	About 4 oz (100–125 g) sugar
About 3/4 pint (4–5 dl) water	1 1/2 tablesp. cornflour

Prepare the fruit, cover with cold water and bring slowly to the boil. As soon as the berries start to break up, add the sugar, stirring until dissolved, and thicken with the cornflour dissolved in a little water. Turn into a dish and sprinkle with sugar to prevent a skin forming.

Serve with cream or milk.

Red fruit jelly
RØDGRØD

Possibly the most popular and well-known Danish sweet of all, this makes use of all the fruits in season right from the end of July until the end of August.

1 lb (500 g) redcurrants	1/2 lb (250 g) blackcurrants	2 1/2–3 tablesp. cornflour per 1
1/2 lb (250 g) cherries or raspberries	5–6 tablesp. sugar About 1 1/2 pint (3/4 l) water	pint liquid (2 1/2–3 tablesp. per 3/4 l.

Wash the berries (there is no need to remove the stalks). Place in layers in an enamel saucepan, adding just enough water to cover. Bring slowly to the boil and simmer until the fruit has all broken up and the juice is dark red in colour.

Sieve the juice through a clean, scalded piece of linen or cheese-cloth, pressing as much juice out of the berries as possible. Measure the juice, boil up and thicken with the required amount of cornflour dissolved in a little cold water.

Pour into a bowl, sprinkle with sugar to prevent a skin forming and serve cold with milk or cream.

Late Summer

In August the light nights of the Danish summer are already over, but the mild late-summer evenings have their special charm.

Fried eels and potatoes in white sauce
STEGT ÅL MED STUVEDE KARTOFLER

For those lucky enough to live by the sea it is still possible to see carbide-lamps over the water at the time of the new moon – a traditional method of catching eels.

3 lb (1¹/₂ kg) eels	1–2 eggs
Flour	2–3 tablesp. water
Salt	Fine breadcrumbs
Ground black	2¹/₂–3 oz (75 g)
pepper	butter

Choose medium-sized eels. Clean and remove the skins, cutting off the tips of the tails.

Cut the fish into about 3 inch (8 cm) pieces, sprinkle with salt and leave for 25–30 min. Dry carefully with kitchen paper and turn in seasoned flour. Dip in beaten egg to which a little water has been added and coat with breadcrumbs.

Brown about 1 oz butter in a very hot pan and fry the eels until golden. Pour off the remainder of the butter in order to extract some of the rather indigestible eel-fat, and add some fresh butter. Turn down the heat and finish frying the eels, turning frequently. This is the traditional way of frying eels, but they may also be turned in seasoned flour and fried as above.

Potatoes in white sauce
STUVEDE KARTOFLER

2 lb (1 kg) potatoes	About 3/4 pint (1/2 l) milk
2 oz (50 g) butter	Salt
2 tablesp. (50 g) flour	Ground white pepper
	Grated nutmeg

Boil the potatoes in their skins, peel and slice. Make a white sauce with the butter, flour and milk, adding just sufficient milk to obtain the desired consistency. Season, and add the potatoes, heating well through before serving.

An easier and less substantial version of the same dish can be made as follows:

2 lb (1 kg) potatoes	About 3/4 pint (1/2 l) coffee cream	Ground white pepper
	Salt	Grated nutmeg

Scrape and peel the potatoes, cut into pieces, boil up, rinse and drain.

Cover with just sufficient cream and cook until tender, by which time the cream sauce should have thickened. Season to taste, taking care not to break up the potatoes. See colourplate opposite the titlepage.

42

Wood pidgeons
SKOVDUER

6 young wood
  pidgeons
Salt
Ground black
  pepper
3–4 oz (100 g)
  butter
6 thin rashers
  very fat fresh
  bacon

1 tablesp. brandy
2–3 tablesp. port
$^1/_2$–$^3/_4$ pint (4–5
  dl) cream
1–2 teasp.
  cornflour
Rowan or
  redcurrant jelly
Watercress

Pluck and clean the pidgeons and singe carefully.
Sprinkle with salt and pepper, place a lump of butter
inside each bird and tie on the fresh bacon rashers.
Brown well on all sides, pour the brandy over the
birds and set alight. Add the port and about ¼ of
the cream and fry the pidgeons over a gentle heat
for 25–35 min. according to size.

Take out the birds, remove the bacon and keep hot.
Boil up the pan with the remainder of the cream until it thickens. If necessary, thicken with a little
cornflour dissolved in cream, season, and add a little
of the jelly to taste.

Serve with small potatoes – cooked in their skins,
peeled and fried in butter, jelly and watercress.

Older birds may be boiled until tender and then fried
in exactly the same way. The difference in result is
almost negligible.

September

A September speciality is the fat, glistening autumn herring – too cheap in Denmark to be valued as much as it should, but by rights just as much a luxury as the eel.

Fried herrings STEGTE SILD

10 large, fresh herrings (about 3 lb or 1¹/₂ kg)	3–4 oz (100 g) butter	Salt 3 lemons
Rye-flour	Ground black pepper	Parsley or dill

Clean and scrape the herrings, rinse and dry with kitchen paper. Fillet if desired, although they are tastier "on the bone". Turn in seasoned rye-flour and **fry** in browned butter about 3–4 min. on each side until golden and crisp.

Serve with boiled potatoes sprinkled with parsley or dill, lemon boats and the remainder of the melted butter.

Herrings in vinegar SILD I EDDIKE

Any left-over herrings are delicious when pickled, decorated with onion rings and served with rye-bread and butter.

44

For the marinade:
3 parts vinegar to
1 part water
Salt

Black peppercorns
Sugar to taste
Onion rings

Boil up the vinegar, water, spices and sugar. Cool, and add the fried herrings. Leave for a day before serving.

Danish meat balls and French beans in white sauce
FRIKADELLER MED STUVEDE SNITTEBØNNER

Another popular dish at this time of the year, French beans in white sauce may be served with Danish meat balls made from the forcemeat used in the recipe for BOM (see page 18). Form the balls with a tablespoon dipped in browned butter, and fry 3–4 min. on each side. They are cooked as soon as they feel firm when pressed with the back of the spoon.

French beans in white sauce
STUVEDE SNITTEBØNNER

$1^1/_2$ lb ($^3/_4$ kg)
French beans
2 oz (50 g)
butter
2 tablesp. (50 g)
flour
About $^3/_4$ pint

(4–5 dl) milk
3–4 tablesp. (1 dl)
cream
Salt
Ground white
pepper
Grated nutmeg

Wash and string the beans, cutting them slantwise into lengths of about 1 inch (2 cm). Steam until tender in salted water. Drain.

Make a white sauce with the butter, flour and milk, boiling well through and adding sufficient cream to obtain the desired consistency. Season and add the beans.

Serve with meat balls and potatoes.

October,
Month of the Chase

In October the true hunting season begins, and the excitement may well spread to the kitchen, because game is universally prized. Game for the Danish housewife includes hare, pheasant, partridge, deer and wild duck.

Roast hare
STEGT HARE

1 large hare	Salt
About ¹/₂ pint (3 dl) stock	Sage
	8–10 rashers fat fresh bacon
About 2 oz (50 g) butter	³/₄ pint (4–5 dl) cream
Ground black pepper	Soy Sauce

Examine the prepared hare carefully, removing any sinews. Cut off the front legs, tying the back legs to the body. Sprinkle with salt, pepper and a little sage, rub with butter and cover with the bacon rashers, securing with string.

Roast on a grid in a roasting-pan at about 440° F (225° C) for 15–20 min. until brown. Pour in the boiling stock until it almost reaches the grid. Roast for about 30–40 min. at about 350° F (180° C) until done (when the legs are tender the hare is cooked). The front legs may also be cooked during the second stage of the roasting – they then become tender without drying up.

Boil up the gravy from the pan with the cream, seasoning with salt, pepper, a little sage and soy sauce.

Serve with small potatoes (boiled in their skins, peeled and browned in butter), rowan jelly and watercress.

Pheasant and green grapes
FASAN MED GRØNNE DRUER

This recipe comes from Åbenrå in the south of Jutland, and is a true October delicacy.

3 pheasants	Salt	3 thin rashers fat
2 lb (1 kg) green	Ground black	fresh bacon
grapes	pepper	1/2–3/4 pint (4–5
Aquavit	4–5 oz (125 g)	dl) cream
(preferably	butter	1 pot sour cream
Brøndum's)		Soy Sauce

The day before the pheasant is to be served, halve the grapes, remove the seeds and cover with aquavit.

Singe the plucked and cleaned pheasants. Rub the insides with salt and pepper and stuff with grapes. Rub the outsides with butter, sprinkle with salt and pepper and cover with the bacon rashers, securing with string.

Brown in butter on all sides in a heavy saucepan. Add a little water and the remaining grapes, breaking them up with a spoon. Add half the cream and simmer under a tightly-fitting lid for about 1–1½ hours depending on age, basting frequently and add-

48

ing more liquid if necessary. When the legs are cooked the birds are done. Take them out and keep warm. Boil up the gravy with the remainder of the cream and the sour cream to taste. Season with salt, pepper, soy sauce and perhaps a little rowan jelly.

Divide the birds into equal pieces and cover with a little of the gravy. Serve with small boiled potatoes and rowan jelly.

Cook sooner too many pheasants than too few – the remainder can be served as a stew the following day, crumbling a little Danish Blue cheese into the gravy – a great treat! Lastly, do not forget the aquavit the grapes have been soaking in!

Sailor's stew SKIPPERLABSKOVS

October is often cold and damp in Denmark, and a substantial dish that can be served with beer and snaps may be very welcome.

1 lb (½ kg) stewing beef	12–15 peppercorns Salt	Finely chopped parsley
2 lb (1 kg) potatoes	Butter for frying About 7 oz (200 g) cooked ham if desired	Worcestershire Sauce
2 large onions		
3–4 bay leaves		

Cut the beef into ¾ inch (2 cm) squares, blanch and rinse in cold water. Chop the onions finely, peel and cut up the potatoes.

Brown 2 tablesp. butter in a thick-buttomed saucepan,

OPPOSITE: *Yellow Pea Soup (p. 54).*

turn the meat in the butter until just coloured. Add the onions and simmer until transparent. Add the potatoes, bay leaves and peppercorns, and cover with water. Simmer gently until all the potatoes have mashed up.

Traditionally about 7 oz chopped ham may be added just before serving.

Season with salt and serve with a lump of butter, finely chopped parsley and Worcestershire Sauce.

Cones with whipped cream
KRÆMMERHUSE MED FLØDESKUM

3 large eggs	2 tablesp. (¹/₂ dl)
4 oz (100 g) sugar	water or beer
4 oz (100 g) flour	Seeds from ¹/₂
	vanilla pod

Mix the ingredients to form a fairly soft dough, and drop on to a well-greased baking sheet with a large teaspoon, leaving plenty of room between each. Flatten out into round, thin cakes with a palette-knife. Bake at 360° F (200° C) for 7–8 minutes. Form into cones while still warm and cool in bottle-necks.

November, and Christmas on the Way

In November the festive season starts again with Martinmas Eve on the tenth of the month.

Roast goose STEGT GÅS

Many Danish homes celebrate Martinmas with the traditional roast goose.

1 goose (about 12–13 lb or 5¹/₂–6 kg)	*1 lb (¹/₂ kg) sour apples*	*1 glass red wine*
Salt	*¹/₂ lb (¹/₄ kg) stoneless prunes*	*Soy Sauce*
Ground black pepper	*¹/₄–¹/₂ pint (2¹/₂ dl) stock*	*3–4 tablesp. cream*
		Cornflour for thickening

Dry the prepared goose carefully inside with kitchen paper and rub with salt and pepper. Peel and quarter the apples, removing the core. Scald the prunes in boiling water and stuff the goose with the apples and prunes. Rub the outside with kitchen salt.

Put the goose on a grid in a roasting-pan with the breast uppermost and place in a cold oven set at 220° F (160° C) and roast for 45 minutes. Pour in a little cold water and roast the goose for 3¹/₂–4 hours according to size and age, taking care not to let the water dry up. When the legs are tender the goose is cooked.

Pour the gravy from the pan and replace the goose in the oven. Pour 2 tablesp. cold water over the breast and increase the heat to 480° F (250° C), leaving the oven door ajar.

Skin the fat off the gravy and set aside for goose dripping. Boil up the gravy with the stock and red wine, season plentifully with salt, pepper and soy sauce and add cream to taste.

Serve with boiled potatoes, browned in sugar, white potatoes, sweet pickles and Danish red cabbage.

Danish red cabbage
RØDKÅL

1 red cabbage (about 3 lb or 1½ kg)	or 1 tablesp. vinegar
2 oz (50 g) butter	About ¼ pint (1½–2 dl)
2–3 teasp. sugar	cherry or
Juice of ½ lemon	blackcurrant juice

Remove the outermost leaves of the cabbage and quarter the remainder, removing the stem. Shred finely.

Melt the butter, stir in the sugar over a gentle heat, add the lemon juice, a little of the fruit juice and boil up together. Put in the cabbage and turn in the liquid. Cover and steam until tender for about 2 hours, stirring frequently and adding more fruit juice if necessary.

Remove the lid for the last 15 minutes, add a lump of butter and more lemon juice and sugar to taste.

Many Danish people like to add a few caraway seeds or a few slices of apple to the cabbage.

Danish apple cake ÆBLEKAGE

Martinmas Goose and Danish Apple Cake are almost inseparable partners.

3 lb (1¹/₂ kg) apples – not too sweet	10 oz (300 g) dried breadcrumbs	¹/₄–¹/₂ pint (2¹/₂ dl) whipping cream
10 oz (300 g) sugar	7 oz (200 g) butter	

Peel and halve the apples, removing the core. Slice thinly – do *not* place in cold water to preserve the colour.

Grease an oven-proof dish and line with a layer of breadcrumbs. Dot with lumps of butter, sprinkle with sugar to taste and cover with a thick layer of apples. Repeat until all is used up, finishing with a layer of breadcrumbs. Press well together, dot with butter and bake at 330° F (165° C) for about 30 minutes until the apples are cooked through.

Cool and turn out of the form, decorating with whipped cream when quite cold. The apple cake may also be served luke-warm with whipped cream.

Roast duck STEGT AND

Many Danish people prefer duck for Martinmas Eve. It has a more delicate flavour and is less fat.

1 duck (4–5 lb for 4 persons or 2–2¹/₂ kg)	¹/₂ lb (250 g) sour apples	stock
		Soy Sauce
Salt	¹/₄ lb (125 g) stoneless prunes	3–4 tablesp. cream
Ground black pepper	About ³/₄ pint (3¹/₂–4 dl)	Cornflour for thickening

Prepare in exactly the same way as the goose, placing it in a cold oven. Set the oven at 220° F (160° C) and, after about 45 min., pour in the bouillon and continue roasting for another 1½ hours. Turn up the heat to 440° F (225° C) and roast for about 20 min. to finish.

Pour off the gravy. Prepare and serve as for the goose.

Yellow pea soup GULE ÆRTER

This is another November dish, much prized in Denmark and often used for festive occasions, served with a glass of ice-cold snaps. It is much improved in flavour when prepared a day in advance.

1½ lb (¾ kg) split yellow peas	2–3 pig's hocks	bouquet garni
2 beef marrow bones	2 lb (1 kg) boiling fresh bacon or pork	1 onion
		2–3 carrots
	1 bunch herbs or	1 parsnip
		Salt

Soak the split peas in cold, boiled water overnight. The next day, bring to the boil and simmer gently until soft, stirring to prevent them from burning. Pass through a sieve or blend in a mixer.

Bind together some celery leaves, 2–3 sprays parsley, 1 bay leaf, 1 spray thyme, a little lovage and the top of a leek, and place the bunch of herbs together with the vegetables and the meat in 6–7 pints (3½–4 l) cold, slightly salted water. Bring slowly to the boil and simmer until the meat is tender, removing the scum from time to time. Cool.

The finished peas

4 leeks	2 lb (1 kg) salted
5–6 carrots	saddle of pork
1 celeriac	1 lb (¹/₂ kg)
¹/₂ lb (250 g)	German
shallots	mettwurst, or
1 bunch thyme	similar type of
	sausage

Removing the top layer of fat, sieve the soup and boil together with the prepared vegetables, which should be removed as soon as tender and cut up into small squares (with the exception of the onions).

Boil up a bunch of thyme with the soup until it has imparted the desired flavour. Gradually add the soup to the pea purée until the required thickness is obtained, and then add the vegetables.

Cover the salt pork with cold water, bring slowly to the boil and simmer 20–30 min. If cooked too long it will become tough. Boil the mettwurst together with the pork for the last 10–12 min., first pricking it with a fork.

Serve the very hot peas together with the cold bacon, hot salt pork and sausage, rye-bread and mustard, not forgetting the cold snaps. See colourplate opposite page 49.

Cap this festive dish with pancakes.

√ **Pancakes**
(about 16)
PANDEKAGER

3 whole eggs	3–4 tablesp. stout
3–4 tablesp.	3¹/₂ oz (100 g)
buttermilk	melted butter
1¹/₂–2 tablesp.	Salt
sugar	Cardamom
7 oz (200 g) plain	Grated rind of 1
flour	lemon
¹/₂ pint (2 dl)	Strawberry or
whipping cream	gooseberry jam

Beat together the eggs, buttermilk and sugar and stir in the flour, stout and half the cream. Flavour with salt, cardamom and lemon-peel and leave for about 30 minutes.

Melt the butter, cool and stir into the batter. Whip the remainder of the cream and fold in gently.

Fry the pancakes in a hot pan. Butter is needed to fry the first pancake only, since the batter itself contains butter.

✓ Meat soup with vegetables and dumplings
OKSEKØDSUPPE MED KØDBOLLER OG MELBOLLER

This is a good dish for the end of November – before the Christmas season starts.

4–5 lb (2–2¹/₂ kg) stewing beef (lean breast or tail)	Salt	3–4 leeks
	1 peeled onion stuck with 2 cloves	1 bunch herbs (celery tops, bay leaf,
2–3 marrow bones	1 small celeriac	parsley, thyme,
5–6 pints (3–3¹/₂ l) water	3–4 carrots	lovage and leek top)
	1 parsley root	

Boil a clean linen cloth and wring dry. Wipe the meat and bones clean and cover with cold water. Bring slowly to the boil, removing the scum.

Add the bunch of herbs and the prepared vegetables, except the leeks. Remove the vegetables as soon as they are tender, excepting the herbs and onions.

Simmer until the meat is tender (about 2¹/₂–3 hours), but not too long, otherwise it will become tough. Boil the bones in the soup an extra 45 minutes–1 hour, and sieve through a scalded linen cloth or cheese-cloth. If the soup still requires clearing, leave it to cool, beat 3–4 egg-whites together with a little cold water and beat into the soup. Bring slowly to the boil, beating constantly, and simmer for 10 min., then the egg-white will have collected all the impurities and formed a layer on the surface. Remove this layer when cool and use it for pet-food.

Leave the soup to stand until the next day and remove any fat globules by drawing a piece of kitchen paper over the surface. Heat it up again and add the well-washed, finely sliced leeks and simmer for 3–4 min. until tender. Add the remainder of the sliced vegetables and serve the soup with meat balls and dumplings. The meat balls are made of forcemeat (see page 18) dropped with a teaspoon into salted boiling water.

Dumplings
MELBOLLER

4 oz (120 g)	1/4–1/2 pint
butter	(2–2 1/2 l) water
4 oz (120 g) flour	4 eggs
	Salt

Make a light roux of the butter and flour, adding as much water as the dough can take – it should be smooth and slip the spoon when removed from the heat. Cool and beat in the eggs one at a time. Season to taste.

Drop the dumplings – not too many at a time – into plenty of salted boiling water. Leave in the nearly boiling water for 3–4 min. and then plunge them into ice-cold water. As soon as they fall to the bottom, they are done. Dumplings should never be allowed to boil, or they break up, and thus should never be boiled up in the soup.

This portion gives about 100 dumplings, but since they are very suitable for freezing, it is an excellent idea to make an extra large quantity and freeze some down.

Horseradish sauce PEBERRODSSOVS

The beef the soup is made from deserves to be eaten with horseradish sauce.

2 oz (50 g) butter	3 oz (75 g)	Sugar to taste
2 oz (50 g) flour	currants	Salt
1¼ pint (¾ l) soup	1–1½ tablesp. vinegar	Freshly grated horseradish

Make a white sauce with the butter, flour and soup. Add the vinegar to taste, and the sugar, salt and horseradish. The sauce should be strongly flavoured. Finally, add the washed and scalded currants. Slice the meat and warm up in the sauce, which should not be allowed to boil once the horseradish has been added.

Serve with boiled, preferably rather floury, potatoes.

The Month of Christmas

From start to finish December is a festive month, right in the darkest period of the year. Christianity was introduced into Denmark during the reign of Harald Bluetooth (950–985 A.D.), but before then, like in so many other countries, we used to celebrate the solstitial festivals.

But, to turn to the more prosaic side of Christmas, here is a traditional recipe.

Brown cookies BRUNE KAGER

These make a good start to the Christmas recipes, because the dough has to be left for at least 14 days before baking.

1 lb (450 g) treacle	1 oz bitter orange peel	cardamom
9 oz (250 g) butter	1 tablesp. cinnamon	1 teasp. baking powder
9 oz (250 g) brown sugar	1 tablesp. ground cloves	2 tablesp. rosewater
	1/2 teasp.	2 lb (1 kg) flour
		Almonds

Warm the syrup in a saucepan, add the butter, orange peel, spices and sugar. Stir in the baking powder, dissolved in the rosewater. Gradually add the flour, kneading thoroughly after each addition. Turn into a bowl, cover with a cloth and keep cold.

Before baking, roll out thinly and cut into rounds. Place well apart on a greased baking-sheet, brush with water and decorate with sliced almonds. Bake for 8–10 min. at 400° F (200° C).

According to custom, the whole family should taste the dough the day it is made in order to bring good luck. At the same time each member should make a wish – and keep it secret, or it will not come true.

Smalls KLEJNER

Smalls are so much a part of Christmas that the baking itself forms part of the celebrations.

3 eggs	1/4 lb (125 g)	2 tablesp. brandy
1/2 lb (250 g)	butter	1 lb (500 g) flour
sugar	5 tablesp. cream	

Beat the eggs and sugar together until white and fluffy. Melt and cool the butter, and add together with the cream and brandy. Mix in the flour and knead well, leaving overnight.

Roll out the dough thinly and cut into diamond shapes with a pastejagger or a sharp knife. Make a slit in the middle of each diamond and pull one of the corners through the slit.

Deep-fry in boiling fat until golden, and drain on absorbent paper.

Rice pudding RISENGRØD

Traditional Danish Christmas dinner consists of rice pudding followed by roast goose. Nowadays many families prefer roast pork or duck and ris à l'amande (see page 63), which is not quite so heavy.

¹/₂ lb (225 g) pudding rice	*¹/₂–³/₄ pint (3¹/₂–4 dl) cream*
2–3 pints (1¹/₂ l) water	*Salt*

Boil the rice in the water for about 25 min. until soft. Gradually add the cream and flavour with salt. This method makes a lighter pudding, and it is less likely to burn on to the saucepan.

Serve with a lump of butter, cinnamon and sugar. In Denmark a sweet, non-alcoholic beer known as Christmas or Yule brew accompanies this dish.

Goose and duck

(see page 51 and 53)

Roast pork
FLÆSKESTEG

5–6 lb (2¹/₂ kg) leg of pork	*Colman's mustard*
About ¹/₃ pint (2¹/₂ dl) stock	*4–6 tablesp. cream*
	1 tablesp. tomato purée
Salt	*Soy Sauce*
Ground black pepper	*Cornflour for thickening*

Score the pork and rub with salt, mustard powder and a little pepper. Place on a grid and roast at 480° F (250° C) for about ¹/₂ hour or until the crackling turns white. Turn the oven down to 360° F (180° C) and pour in the boiling stock.

Roast the joint for a further 2¼ hours depending on the size. Do not baste, or the crackling will become soft, but turn down the heat if it becomes too dark. Pour the gravy into a small saucepan, leaving the joint to keep hot in the oven with the door ajar. Skim the fat off the gravy and add the cream to taste. Boil up with the salt, pepper, tomato pureé and soy sauce, thickening with cornflour if desired.

Serve with Danish red cabbage (see page 52), browned potatoes (see page 28) and sweet pickle.

Roast saddle of pork may be preferred to the leg as a Christmas joint, and needs only 1½–1¾ hours roasting time. For a fatter joint, choose neck of pork, but remember that if the crackling is to become crisp it has to be soft and elastic when raw. See colourplate opposite page 64.

Red cabbage salad RØDKÅLSSALAT

Fat joints are often served with red cabbage salad – a lighter alternative to the traditional boiled red cabbage.

½ red cabbage	1 tablesp. water	Freshly grated
2–3 tablesp. lemon	5–6 tablesp. olive	horseradish
juice	oil	Sugar to taste

Quarter the cabbage and remove the stem. Shred finely.

Mix the above ingredients to make the dressing. Pour over the cabbage and leave for an hour before serving, tossing at intervals.

Serve cold with the hot joint.

Ris à l'amande

An alternative to the traditional rice pudding.

4 oz (120 g)
Patna rice
1¼ pints (¾ l)
water
½ vanilla pod

½–¾ pint (3–4
dl) whipping
cream
3–3½ oz (75–100
g) finely
chopped
almonds

2 tablesp. sugar
Tinned or bottled
cherries

Cook the rice in the water until tender, together with
the vanilla seeds and sugar. Stir in half the cream
and the chopped almonds. Whip the rest of the cream
and fold into the mixture.
Serve cold with preserved cherries.
No matter whether rice pudding or ris à l'amande is
preferred, it is customary to hide a whole almond in
the rice. The lucky finner then receives the "almond
prize" – anything from chocolate or a bottle of wine
to a book.

Christmas goodies JULEKNAS

Walnuts, hazelnuts, almonds, Brazil nuts, small red
apples, mandarins or clementines, dates, figs, raisins,
oranges and marzipan confectionary traditionally
complete Christmas dinner.

Christmas Lunch

Danish Christmas lunch is just as important as the preceding dinner, and is usually held on Christmas or Boxing Day. Many restaurants serve this resplendent Cold Table during the week before Christmas.

The following recipes for Christmas lunch may also be extended to other times of the year.

Pickled herrings
MARINEREDE SILD

	About 4 oz (100–125 g) sugar	1 small carrot, finely sliced
	1½ tablesp. whole allspice	3 pieces whole ginger
4 salted herring fillets	1 tablesp. Colman's mustard	1–3 bay leaves
¾ pint (4 dl) vinegar		2 teasp. white peppercorns
3–4 tablesp. water	Small piece of horseradish	2–3 red onions or dill

Soak the herrings in water or milk for 8–10 hours, or until as salty as desired.

Boil up the remaining ingredients (excepting the onion or dill) in the water and vinegar and cool. Cut the herring fillets slantwise into about 1 inch (2 cm) pieces and cover with the cold liquid. Leave for 18–24 hours. Decorate with finely sliced onion rings or chopped dill before serving.

OPPOSITE: *Roast Pork (p. 61) with Potatoes Browned in Sugar (p. 28). In the background: Ris à l'Amande (p. 63).*

Salt herrings in mustard sauce
SENNEPSSILD

4 salt herring fillets	1 tablesp. sweet mustard
1 tablesp. white wine vinegar	1 tablesp. dark French mustard
2 tablesp. sour cream	About 15 white peppercorns
3–4 tablesp. olive oil	1–2 bunches dill

Prepare the herrings as in the last recipe, but cut into smaller pieces and lay them like whole fillets on a flat dish.

Beat together the vinegar, mustard and sour cream, and gradually add the oil until the consistency is that of thin mayonnaise. Season with the crushed peppercorns and pour over the herring fillets.

Decorate with freshly chopped dill, or stir a little dried dill into the sauce.

Herring salad
SILDESALAT

2 salted herring fillets	Ground white pepper
The same quantity of pickled beetroot and sour apples	Colman's mustard
	1/2 pickled ridge cucumber
Cucumber vinegar	Beetroot vinegar
Salt	Mayonnaise

Soak the herring fillets to remove the surplus salt, and place them in the cucumber vinegar. Leave for 18–24 hours. Cut the herrings and beetroot and sour apple into fine strips.

Flavour the mayonnaise with the spices, the cucumber (mashed through a parsley mill) and the beetroot vinegar. The mayonnaise should be just thick enough to bind the filling, and very strongly spiced.

Curry salad
KARRYSILD

2 salted herring fillets	Chopped whites of 4 eggs
The same quantity of cooked tongue or ham	Mayonnaise Curry
2–3 tablesp. cream	Ground white pepper

Blend the mayonnaise with the cream until soft, and season with the curry powder and pepper.

Soak the herring fillets to remove the surplus salt and chop finely. Add them to the mayonnaise together with the finely chopped meat. Leave in a cold place for a couple of hours and season again if necessary.

Just before serving, add the chopped egg-whites and decorate with hard-boiled and quartered yolks.

Luncheon meat balls
FROKOSTFRIKADELLER

1 portion
forcemeat
(see page 18)

The forcemeat may be spiced with curry or paprika to add a piquant flavour. Form with a teaspoon and fry in browned butter until cooked through. Serve hot.

Roast tenderloin of pork

HELSTEGTE MØRBRAD

3 pork tenderloins (or 2 veal tenderloins)	Dried fennel
	Butter for frying
	2 tablesp. water
Salt	3–4 tablesp. cream
Ground black pepper	4–5 onions
	Soy sauce

Clean the tenderloins, removing the sinews, beat lightly with the fists and sprinkle with salt, pepper and fennel. Brown in a pan with plenty of butter, add the water and cream, cover, and simmer for about 6–7 min. Take out the meat and place in an oven-proof dish.

Meanwhile, peel and chop the onions finely and brown in butter until just golden, adding a little water to keep them soft. Boil up the onions in the gravy from the meat, adding a little more liquid if necessary. Season with salt, pepper and soy sauce.

Pour the onion sauce over the meat, place on an asbestos mat, cover with a tightly-fitting lid and simmer until tender over a gentle heat.

Bacon and apples

ÆBLEFLÆSK

20–30 rashers of lean fresh bacon	3 lb (1½ kg) apples

Fry the fresh bacon in a roasting-pan in the oven at 340° F (160° C) until crisp. Pour off the fat at intervals.

Quarter the apples, removing the core, and cook them until soft in the bacon-fat – adding sugar to taste. Place the bacon and apple in an oven-proof dish and serve with rye-bread.

Liver paste
LEVERPOSTEJ

1½ lb (700 g) pig's liver	2 eggs
	Salt
10 oz (300 g) suet	Ground black
2 oz (50 g) butter	pepper
2 oz (50 g) flour	Powdered thyme
¾ pint (4 dl) milk	or marjoram

Pass the liver and the suet separately through the mincer a couple of times.

Make a Béchamel sauce with the butter, flour and milk and melt in the suet very slowly, stirring constantly.

Cool and stir in the chopped liver. Season with the salt, pepper, and thyme or marjoram and beat in the eggs one at a time.

Bake in the oven in a water-bath at 350° F (175° C) for about 1 hour until set.

When raw the liver paste is very suitable for freezing down, and may be placed in the oven directly from the freezer and baked 1– 1½ hours at 340° F (170° C).

Brawn SYLTE

This belongs to the traditional Christmas table.

1 pig's head with ears	Ground black pepper
1–2 hocks	Allspice
Salt	

Wash the pig's head and hocks, divide into pieces, scrape and cover with cold salted water. Bring to the boil, removing the scum, and cook until very tender (2¹/₂–3 hours). Leave to cool.

Take out the meat, slice off the skin finely and line a dish with the skin and ears – the latter are regarded as a great delicacy. Remove the meat and fat from the bones, cut into cubes and mix well together.

Place a layer of meat and fat in the bowl, sprinkle with a mixture of salt, pepper and allspice, and repeat until the bowl is full.

Strain the soup, boil up and pour over the meat until covered. Press lightly and leave in a cold place until set. Turn out on to a dish and serve with rye-bread, strong mustard and pickled beetroot.

Chitterlings
FINKER

1 pig's kidney	Thyme
1 pig's liver	3–4 bay leaves
1 pig's heart	Salt
The same quantity of suet	Ground black pepper
15 shallots	Worcestershire Sauce
2 large, sour apples	

Clean the offal and boil until tender together with the shallots, thyme and bay leaves.

Mince the suet and melt down very slowly to form greaves. Pour off half the fat and fry up the finely sliced apple in the pan with the greaves.

Meanwhile chop up the offal finely, mix with the greaves and season with salt and pepper. Cook well through, season again if necessary and add a little Worcestershire Sauce. Serve with rye-bread.

Pig's trotters
GRISETÆER

3–4 pig's trotters
Salt
15–20 white
   peppercorns
4 bay leaves

Gelatine
1 sliced onion
Vinegar
Water

Split the pig's trotters, scrub, scrape and scald. Cover with 1 part of vinegar to 2 parts water, adding the remaining ingredients, and boil up. Remove the scum, and simmer until tender for about 2–3 hours, removing any further scum during the cooking.

Place the trotters in a dish. Boil up the soup and stiffen with gelatine according to the instructions on the packet, and pour into the dish to cover the trotters.

Serve with rye-bread and lemon or vinegar.

Pickled beetroots
SYLTEDE RØDBEDER

2 lb (1 kg)
   beetroots
1¹/₂ pint (³/₄ l)
   vinegar
About 7 oz (200
   g) sugar
2–3 thin slices

horseradish
1 tablesp. pickling
   spices
Preservative –
   follow the
   instructions on
   the bottle

Cook the beetroots until tender, rub off the skins and slice thinly. Lay the slices in a scalded jar. Boil up the vinegar with sugar and spices, remove from the heat and add the preservative. Pour over the beetroots.

Leave to stand for a few days before serving.

South Jutland sour rib
SØNDERJYSK SURRIB

12–16 rashers fresh bacon	15–20 peppercorns
Gelatine (see the instructions on the packet)	4 bay leaves
	1 slice onion
	Vinegar
Salt	Water

Cut off the bacon-rinds, cover the bacon with 1 part vinegar to 2 parts water, add the onions and spices and boil for about 15 min. Lay the bacon rashers in a dish.

Skim and sieve the liquid and boil up. Stiffen with the gelatine dissolved in a little water and pour over the bacon. Leave to cool before serving with rye-bread, vinegar or lemon. See colourplate opposite titlepage.

And, moreover,
the Danish Christmas table also includes rolled, spiced cold meat, salami, boiled tongue, Italian salad and a few good cheeses.

New Year

On the last evening of the old year it is customary to eat boiled cod – and very welcome it is too, on top of all the fat Christmas fare.

Boiled cod
KOGT TORSK

8–10 large slices cod	Freshly grated horseradish
Salt	4–6 hard-boiled eggs
Butter	
Fish mustard	

Cover the cod with salty water and bring slowly to the boil. Simmer for 2 min., cover and remove from the heat. After 12 min. the cod should be cooked.
Serve with melted butter, fish mustard, finely grated horseradish and chopped, hard-boiled egg. Some people prefer to blend the horseradish in the melted butter and the fish mustard in a light sauce (see recipe for hard-boiled eggs in mustard sauce, page 22).

Danish doughnuts ÆBLESKIVER
Finally, a recipe for doughnuts, which are eaten both at Christmas and New Year – although they taste equally delicious at any other time of the year.

72

¹/₄–¹/₂ pint (2¹/₂ dl) cream	3–4 tablesp. stout	1 teasp. lemon juice
¹/₂ lb (250 g) flour	1 tablesp. sugar	¹/₂ teasp. cardamom
4 eggs	6 oz (175 g) butter	

Beat the cream and flour together and beat in the egg-yolks one at a time. Stir in the stout, sugar and cooled, melted butter. Flavour with lemon juice and stir in the stiffly beaten egg-whites.

Allow to stand for a while.

Place a little butter in the hollows of a doughnut pan (the butter is necessary for the first batch only), and fry the doughnuts, turning on all sides until brown.

Serve hot, sprinkled with icing sugar. See colourplate opposite titlepage.

These doughnuts make a fitting end to the year and bring our little book about seasonal Danish cookery to a close. We hope it will inspire our readers to try for themselves, and recreate some of the meals they may recollect having enjoyed in Denmark.

Index, English

Index, Danish